SPIDER

LIVING THINGS

SPIDER

Rebecca Stefoff

BENCHMARK BOOKS

MARSHALL CAVENDISH
NEW YORK

Benchmark Books
Marshall Cavendish Corporation
99 White Plains Road
Tarrytown, New York 10591

Library of Congress Cataloging-in-Publication Data
Stefoff, Rebecca.
Spider / by Rebecca Stefoff.
p.   cm. — (Living things)
Includes index.
Summary: Examines the physical characteristics, life cycle, and
natural habitat of various kinds of spiders with emphasis on
their ability to extrude silk and weave webs.
ISBN 0-7614-0442-2 (lib. bdg.)
1. Spiders—Juvenile literature. 2. Spider webs—Juvenile literature.
[1. Spiders. 2. Spider webs.] I. Title. II. Series: Stefoff, Rebecca   Living things.
QL458.4.S72   1999   595.4'4—dc21   97-9131   CIP   AC

Photo research by Ellen Barrett Dudley

Cover photo: *The National Audubon Society Collection/Photo Researchers, Inc.*,
Tom McHugh

The photographs in this book are used by permission and through the courtesy of:
Peter Arnold, Inc.: Helga Lade, 2; S.J. Krasemann, 7; Hans Pfletschinger, 10, 19,
(top right), 20, 25 (top and bottom); Ed Reschke, 11, 32; Norbert Wu, 12 {top};
Kevin Schafer, 12 (bottom). *The National Audubon Society Collection/Photo
Researchers, Inc.*: Peter Skinner, 6-7; Harry Rogers, 8; Mark N. Brelton, 9 (top
left); C.K. Lorenz, 9 (bottom); Robert Noonan, 10 (inset); Alan L. Detrick, 13 (left);
Nuridsany et Perennou, 15; Ken Brate, 18 (left); Dr. Paul A. Zahl, 22 (left and right);
Dan Suzio, 24; J.H. Carmichael, 26-27. *Animals Animals*: J.H. Robinson, 9 (top
right), 14; Patti Murray, 13 (right); Stephen Dalton, 16-17; K.G. Preston-Mafham, 17
(inset); Zig Leszczynski, 18-19; J.A.L. Cooke, 19 (bottom); H.L. Fox, 21 (left);
Oxford Scientific Films/John Cooke, 21 (right); Oxford Scientific Films/David G.
Fox, 23.
Printed in Hong Kong

1   3   5   6   4   2

For Kate Nunn, with many thanks

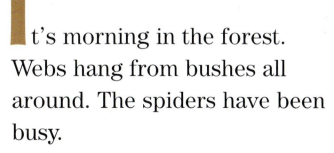

It's morning in the forest. Webs hang from bushes all around. The spiders have been busy.

In the middle of its web, a spider waits. . . .

six-spotted fishing spider

Do you see something crawling by? Is it a spider? Here's how you can tell: All spiders have eight legs. A spider can have long legs or short legs, hairy legs or smooth legs. But it always has eight legs.

two web-building spiders   jumping spider

long-jau ed orb weaver

spinnerets of orb weaver

Spiders can do something wonderful. On their stomachs are spinnerets. These special parts of their bodies make many tiny white threads. Together these threads make a strong, stretchy strand of spider silk. A spider can climb up and down this gossamer strand. Or a spider can walk across its tightrope of silk like a small circus acrobat.

shamrock orb weaver

Some spiders use their silk to make webs. First they attach corner threads to trees, flowers, or houses. Then they spend hours weaving their silk into beautiful designs. Squares, circles, diamonds—spiders make webs in all kinds of shapes.

Some webs last for days or even weeks. Some come apart and must be rebuilt every night. And when the spider has finished making its web, it sits and waits.

Spiderwebs are sticky. When an insect brushes against the web, it sticks. The harder it tries to get away, the more silk gets stuck to it. The spider feels its web jerking and scurries up to wrap the trapped insect in *more* silk.

Argiope, or garden spider, with butterfly

Argiope wrapping captured cricket

These garden spiders have caught a butterfly and a cricket. They will store the insects for a while and then eat them. Once an insect blunders into a spider's web, it will probably never get out again.

Not all spiders build webs and wait for food to be trapped in them. Some are hunters. They stalk their prey and then pounce on it. The jumping spider is hoping to catch that fat bee on the yellow flower.

Have you ever seen a cowboy lasso a calf with a rope? Some spiders do the same thing. They throw loops of silk over flies and other insects.

Even jumping spiders use silk to wrap up their prey. Look closely at the spider that has caught a tree frog. Do you see the fine white threads by the frog's eye? They are the spider's silk.

Jumping spider pounces on fly. (inset): spider eats tree frog.

Some hunting spiders sit quietly, waiting for a tasty bug to wander by.

Can you spot the three spiders in the top row of pictures? All of them are colored to blend into their backgrounds. This is called camouflage. It helps spiders hide from their prey—and also from birds, snakes, and other creatures that might eat them. The crab spider in the bottom picture will "disappear" as soon as it moves from the green leaf onto a yellow flower.

giant crab spider

Eurasian water spider making air bubble . . .

. . . in air bubble . . .   *. . . and with captured minnow*

Silk is a wonderful thing. It even lets one kind of spider live underwater. The spider spins a bell, or bubble, of silk just below the surface of the water. Then it fills this bell with many tiny air bubbles. Now the spider can stay underwater for a long time. Whenever it needs air, it crawls into the bubble to breathe. When it catches a minnow, it takes the prey into the bubble and eats it there.

The trap-door spider digs a snug underground nest. Then it lines its burrow with smooth, soft silk.

A lid of dirt, held together with silk, closes the burrow. When the spider wants to go out, it flips the lid open, climbs out, and then closes it again. From outside, the lid looks like just another piece of the ground. Unless you saw the door opening or closing, you would never know a spider lived there. But many trap-door spiders come out only at night.

. . . and crawls outside.

Mother spiders find still another use for silk when it is time for them to lay their eggs. They spin cases of silk to hold the tiny eggs. Sometimes an egg case holds more than a thousand eggs.

Garden spiders attach their egg cases to sticks or stones and then leave them, never to see them again.

Wolf spiders carry their egg cases around. When it is time for the wolf spider's eggs to hatch, the mother spider bites the case open and dozens of little wolf spiderlings tumble out.

wolf spider with egg case

wolf spiderlings hatching

olf spiderlings get a lift for the first ten days of their lives. They ride around on their mother's back until they are big enough to live on their own.

Other kinds of spiders take care of themselves from the moment they hatch. Someday you may see many long threads of silk floating across a meadow or park, drifting gently on the breeze. These threads are little parachutes. Each one is carrying a young spiderling out into the world to start a new life of hunting and spinning.

female wolf spider with egg case and young

A QUICK LOOK AT THE SPIDER

Spiders are not insects. Unlike insects, which have six legs, spiders have eight legs. They belong to a large class of creatures called arachnids (uh RAK nids). Ticks, mites, and scorpions are also arachnids. Spiders differ from all other arachnids in a very important way: They have spinnerets, organs that produce silk thread, on their abdomens.

Spiders live on all continents except Antarctica. All spiders kill or paralyze their prey with venom from their fangs. Scientists have identified more than 35,000 different species, or kinds, of spiders. Only about twenty of these have venom that is dangerous to humans.

Here are six kinds of spiders, along with their scientific names and a few key facts.

TRUE TARANTULA

Lycosa tarentula

(lie COH suh tuh REN tyew luh)

Belongs to wolf spider family. Lives in southern Europe. Not poisonous to humans. Although the name "tarantula" was given to a group of large, hairy spiders found in Central and South America, the true taranatula is not related to these spiders.

MEDITERRANEAN TENT-BUILDING SPIDER

Uroctea durandi

(yew ROK tee uh doo RAN dee)

Resembles a beetle in shape and markings. This may protect spider from predators that don't like to eat beetles. Spider builds tent-shaped silk nest attached to stick, plant, or log. Found in southern Europe.

LONG-NOSED JUMPING SPIDER

Myrmarachne plataleoides
(meer muh RAK neh plah tah lay OH ee dees)
One of about four thousand species of jumping spider.
Long "nose" is really a pair of jaws, each with a long
fang. When attacking prey or fighting other spiders,
spreads jaws wide and unfolds fangs. Lives in Sri
Lanka, an island off the coast of India.

BLACK WIDOW SPIDER

Latrodectus mactans
(lat roh DEK tus MAK tans)
As with many kinds of spiders, male is
smaller than female. Both have red hour-
glass-shaped mark on abdomen. Bite
contains a nerve poison that can make
people sick or kill them (deaths are very
rare). Found in many parts of North
America.

SPINY-BELLIED ORB WEAVER

Gasteracanthus cancriformis
(gas ter uh KANTH us kan kri FOR mis)
Belongs to the large group of orb weavers, spiders that
build the most elaborate webs. Like some other orb
weavers, has bumps, horns, or spines on body. These may
protect the spider from predators by making it harder to
eat or by giving it a confusing, "unspidery" shape.

BIRD-EATING SPIDER
Theraphosa leblondi
(theh ruh FO suh leh BLON dee)
World's largest spider. Body measures up to three and a half inches (9 cm) across, with leg span of up to eleven inches (28 cm). Has been known to capture and feed on birds and small mammals. Lives in northern South America. Belongs to group of American spiders called tarantulas.

Taking Care of the Spider

Spiders help maintain the balance of nature by eating insects and other prey, and also by providing food for birds, lizards, and insects. We can help protect spiders by preserving the many different kinds of natural places where they live. Some spiders, especially tarantulas, have become popular as pets. Before you buy a pet spider, make certain that it does not belong to an endangered species.

Find Out More

Clarke, Penny. *Insects and Spiders*. New York: Franklin Watts, 1995.

Dewey, Jennifer. *Spiders Near and Far*. New York: Dutton Children's Books, 1993.

Fisher, Enid. *Spiders*. Milwaukee: Gareth Stevens, 1996.

Fowler, Allan. *Spiders Are Not Insects*. Danbury, Conn.: Children's Press, 1996.

LaBonte, Gail. *The Tarantula*. Minneapolis: Dillon Press, 1991.

Nielsen, Nancy. *The Black Widow Spider*. New York: Crestwood House, 1990.

Parsons, Alexandra. *Amazing Spiders*. New York: Knopf Books for Young Readers, 1990.

Penny, Malcolm. *Discovering Spiders*. New York: Bookwright Press, 1986.

Robinson, Faye. *Mighty Spiders!* New York: Scholastic, 1996.

Schnieper, Claudia. *Amazing Spiders*. Minneapolis: Carolrhoda Books, 1989.

Index

Rebecca Stefoff has published many books for young readers. Science and environmental issues are among her favorite subjects. She lives in Oregon and enjoys observing the natural world while hiking, camping, and scuba diving.